Praise for Eric W. Gershman's Publications

"Well documented, straight-forward, and easy. . . ."

—John Waggoner
USA Today

"Simply amazing! Fascinating strategies anyone can enjoy. Buy this book!"

—Doug Rogers
Investors Business Daily

"Eric Gershman brings a strong research background to his publications. . . ."

—Lesley Norton
Barron's

". . .remarkably informed, readable, and timely. Leave it to Eric Gershman to find a slew of great deals broken up into readable tips guaranteed to save anyone a bundle. A great resource!"

—Tom Nutile
The Boston Herald

PAY-NOTHING® To Travel Anywhere You Like

Discovered by the
PayNada.com Editors

Great Pines Publishing, Inc.
Vermont, USA

Copies of this book can be obtained from your local bookstore or the
publisher, who can be reached at the address below.

> PayNada.com
> Great Pines Publishing
> Post Office Box 973
> Stowe, VT 05672

You can also contact the publisher online at <http://www.paynada.com>
or by calling, toll free:

(877) Pay-Nothing [729-6684].

Pay-Nothing to Travel Anywhere You Like. Copyright © 1999 by Eric Gershman.
All rights reserved. Printed in Canada.

FIRST EDITION: 1999
Library of Congress Card Catalog Number: 99-62362

ISBN 1-893977-00-5

The PayNada.com Editors . . .

The Paynada.com Editors are a coalition of dollar-crunching professionals residing primarily in Vermont. Steeped in the Yankee tradition of obtaining half off of everything, the editors bring award winning journalistic excellence to these pages.

Led by financial whiz Eric W. Gershman, whose publications have reached over 200 million readers in the last five years, the PayNada.com Editors now produce publications covering travel, home, children's merchandise, garden, health, and scores of other topics. Look for the "Pay-Nothing" series in your local bookstore, online at www.PayNada.com, or call, toll free, 1-877-Pay-Nothing.

Welcome, Pay-Nothing Traveler . . .

The book you hold in your hands is designed to save you tens of thousands of dollars on your future travels. It teaches you, step-by-step, the secrets of the Pay-Nothing Traveler.

When we say "Pay-Nothing," it doesn't simply refer to free merchandise (although there are plenty of these examples). It also refers to items and services that you'll pay so little for, you're likely to boast, "I paid nothing for it." This is our goal. For example, on page 29, we show you how to obtain a $5,000 stateroom on a luxury liner for 25% of the cost—or less.

The premise of this book is no more complicated than taking advantage of free samples at your local supermarket. If a company is sending free, brand-name shampoo or food samples in the mail, why wouldn't an all-inclusive resort offer free vacations? Why shouldn't an airline move you from coach to first class, just for asking?

As you make your way through the world of travel, keep us posted on your success stories. We'll be updating *Pay-Nothing to Travel Anywhere You Like,* so write or e-mail us with your experiences. Any items used in future editions earn you a free book.

Enjoy, and we'll see you on the road!

—Eric Gershman and
The PayNada.com Editors

Contents

Another...

Guide

How to Use This Book . . .

This book is divided into four chapters. You'll get the most out of it by carefully reading Chapter One, "The 10 Secrets of the Pay-Nothing Traveler." It's our expert's guide to cutting travel costs. Follow it, and you'll easily slash thousands of dollars off your annual travel bills.

In Chapter Two, you'll discover 18 items, and each could save you between $1 and $100 in travel benefits. In Chapter Three, you'll learn 22 ways to save between $100 and $1,000. In Chapter Four, each item listed can save you between $1,000 and $10,000.

Check out the "Secrets That Apply" to various pages. They'll tell you which secrets from Chapter 1, "The 10 Secrets of the Pay-Nothing Traveler," deliver the goods fastest—and easiest.

Finally, look for the picture icons at the top right hand side of each page. They'll give you an instant snapshot into the ease, cost, or excitement-factor of each entry. Here are examples:

Chapter 1

The 10 Secrets of the Pay-Nothing Traveler

*On their first travel writing assignment, finding free lodging
proved to be no problem for Rick and Beth.*

THE 10 SECRETS OF THE PAY-NOTHING TRAVELER

Be a Travel Writer

Pay-Nothing Travelers live for free meals, free luxury accommodations, and VIP access for everything from baseline seats in the Astro Dome to box seats at Radio City Music Hall. Want to learn how to join them? Learn the simple rules of becoming an on-again/off-again travel writer.

While plotting your next vacation, plan to write an article/review of the places you stay, eat, and recreate. To be "on assignment," all you need is a publication to write for and a destination to review. This art is mastered quickly, and the benefits are unbelievable.

See page 79 for specific, step-by-step instructions on how to get going. For now, simply acknowledge the fact that you are indeed a travel writer, and work it into every trip you take.

Despite improved security measures, Eric still finds a way to pass off his cooler full of home brew as a carry-on.

THE 10 SECRETS OF THE PAY-NOTHING TRAVELER

Always Travel "On Business"

B usiness people are the bread and butter of the travel industry—for them, reduced rates exist from taxi cab to takeoff. And just because you're traveling with an Igloo cooler and beach chair doesn't mean you can't score the lower fares. Of course, you'll have to ask, and Pay-Nothing Travelers constantly ask for corporate rates and benefits.

The corporate rate can lower your hotel room cost up to 65% (page 61). Even if your trip is only partially for business, the lower fare holds—and trust us, nobody cares. So, whether at the airport, the rental car counter, the train station, or the restaurant, simply refer to being "on business" and collect your benefits.

Late again for another flight, Robin's pathetic song and dance scored him yet another upgrade.

THE 10 SECRETS OF THE PAY-NOTHING TRAVELER

Be an Airline Industry Expert

The Pay-Nothing Traveler is an expert at the airport. He/she skillfully moves from curbside skycaps to ticket agents to the gate without waiting in lines, obtaining every conceivable benefit along the way.

Whether you're looking for a way to land two free round-trip plane tickets (page 90), or just want to get from the East Coast to the West Coast for half-price, become an expert and watch your savings take off. For other sky-high savings, you can travel as a courier (page 78), snuggle up to the consolidators and wholesalers (page 52), or fly with the ever-expanding discount airlines (page 87). Learn our tricks for working ticket agents, and put the bump on last-minute-travel panic (page 70).

*On the redeye to Rangoon, diaper rash
suddenly hit the septuplets behind him,
sending Edward flying for First Class.*

THE 10 SECRETS OF THE PAY-NOTHING TRAVELER

You Are in Constant Need of an Upgrade

The Pay-Nothing Traveler is constantly purchasing at lower rates and being upgraded. With thousands of hotel room (page 48), airline seat (page 47), and car upgrades (page 24) given away every day, learning to upgrade is a vital organ in the anatomy of smart travel.

Of course, you'll need to ask for the upgrade, and Pay-Nothing Travelers constantly query those who are hiding the goods. Next, you'll need a reason why you are deserving. That's where special occasions, health problems (however slight), and phobias go a long way. What's the payoff? Bigger cars, first class airplane seats, free shuttle services, spa access, massages, free meals, and tons of other kingly rewards will all be yours.

After 40 minutes on hold, Gary could no longer tolerate Yanni's greatest hits.

THE 10 SECRETS OF THE PAY-NOTHING TRAVELER

Be a Skilled Complainer

Competition in American business is at an all time high. Terms like "customer satisfaction" and "quality standards" are buzzwords that carry serious weight in big chains and corporations. The Pay-Nothing Traveler takes advantage of this trend by refining complaining skills to the highest level.

Always keep your end-goal in mind—getting what you want and being the first on the list to get it. That means the last airplane seat, the last hotel room, or a replacement product provided well after the warranty expires. The Pay-Nothing Traveler is never angry, only disappointed. What's more, he/she is firm and constantly suggests big-ticket remedies to ease the pain, regardless of the cost to the company in distress.

It doesn't matter whether you are writing a letter to the president of a poorly manufactured product or confronting a customer service representative at 1:00 a.m. in the middle of Kennedy Airport. The trick is to be kind, patient, and very clear on exactly what your complaint is and what compensation will satisfy you. These days, many service personnel have the power to pacify (page 66). Make them feel your loss, and while the other turkeys are yelling their heads off, gobble up the goods.

Special Report

Call for your special report "One Year Past Warranty? No Problem." 1-877-Pay-Nothing

After Grandma had failed to return from a clothing-optional resort, Cindy questioned her career choice as a travel agent.

Be a Travel Agent

Good travel agents receive countless invitations to fabulous destinations all around the world. That's because they routinely send droves of people to their favorite spots. For the Pay-Nothing Traveler, landing a free week in Jamaica (page 77), for example, is similar: organize a few friends, take care of the booking details, and enjoy the all-expense paid status of a travel agent. We'll even show you how you can earn your license as an accredited travel agent in about a week—and collect commissions on your own trips.

Just volunteer to be the planner for the next bachelor party, sorority reunion, kids vacation, or whatever group travel event comes up. Once you've gathered the gang, pick your destination and contact an outfit that books groups and rewards group planning (page 77). Lastly, put your wallet back in your pocket—you won't need it. Not only will you gain the praise of your friends for planning such a great outing, you'll be taking home those great memories yourself, for free.

*Realizing he knew nothing about Mongolian futures,
Rick fell back on his best Ross Perot impersonation.*

THE 10 SECRETS OF THE PAY-NOTHING TRAVELER

You Are an Expert on a Wide Range of Subjects

Experts travel free in exchange for their skills as a speaker or entertainer. The Pay-Nothing Traveler knows that an hour spent discussing anything from crafts to computers (page 81) can win all-expense paid vacations to the world's best locations.

To get started, identify a few subjects or topics you'd like to share with a group. This can include gardening, cooking, or even a knowledge base you've acquired at work. Next, parlay that knowledge into a one-hour seminar and start contacting cruise lines, hotels, and even tourism ministries of exotic countries with your pitch. If nothing else, teaching English to foreign clientele might get you started. The best targets are cruise lines (page 81), resort hotels (page 84), and overseas lecture tour offices (page 86). Learn the lingo and you'll have free vacation offers coming to you in the mail faster than you can act on them.

Special Report

Call for your special report "How to Get Anything You Want."
1-877-Pay-Nothing

Bert never misses the
"Half Off What You Can Carry" Discount.

Love the Frequent Customer Programs

Businesses give away their products and services every day to those whom they believe are their best customers. Pay-Nothing Travelers are always on the best customer lists, be it the frequent flyer program or the two-for-one taco club.

Frequent customer programs don't often base their rules on dollars spent. Rather, they are more concerned with total visits to their establishments. They routinely value demographic information over total purchases, and their applications for club memberships reflect this. Information about customers is so hard to find, and so expensive to gather, they'll adorn you with gifts just for joining. That's why those annoying mailers gives you 5,000 free miles just for signing up.

But frequent customer programs add up to much more than just another way to cash in your chips. They are primary negotiating tools for when you get into a travel bind or come up shortchanged at the donut shop. And with frequent flyer programs, you can even sell your miles and turn them into cash (page 59). Join up, soldier, and win the war of corporate competition!

There wasn't much Bernard wouldn't do for a quick $5.

Tip Before the Service

Pay-Nothing Travelers are the Navy Seals of tipping. For them, skilled tipping gets the un-gettable and does the un-doable (page 29).

Most people tip after the service is provided. Pay-Nothing Travelers, however, know that a well-timed tip before the event can win countless rewards, from free food in a restaurant to a ship's stateroom worth thousands more than the storage sleeper they booked. In short, for every dollar you tip, you can receive 10 times that amount in value (and that's an actual statistic). What's more, it's not only acceptable, it's downright classy (page 29).

Due to an unfortunate spasm, Zach would burst into the Hustle when offering up his seat for an overbooked flight.

THE 10 SECRETS OF THE PAY-NOTHING TRAVELER

Volunteer

When ticket prices for hard-to-see events start to skyrocket, the Pay-Nothing Traveler goes to work—literally. Professional sports championships and other top events (pages 33 and 56) are in constant, often desperate need of good volunteers.

Normally, you can expect duties along the lines of helping VIPs to their seats, pointing ticket-holders in the right direction, or handing out leaflets. After all the hard work, you can enjoy the show or event. Volunteers for exotic resorts might translate or interpret languages or even dance with single women (page 81). For the most part, it is enjoyable work, and you can gain excellent insiders' benefits.

Chapter 2

Save up to $100.00

No Charge for Lift Tickets

Speak Up!

Ski areas are like insurance companies: they lie about the conditions and then chant "Who? Me?" when you put in a complaint. Few people know how to speak up to ski areas—they have us trained to accept broken ski lifts, wind holds, and stolen skis. Not so for the Pay-Nothing Traveler. While most ski areas can't even spell r-e-f-u-n-d, here's how to get the gold when the white's got you raging red.

◆ If you find yourself stuck on a chair lift for more than 10 minutes, drop by the skier services desk at the end of the day and tell them all about the runs you missed and the cold temperatures you endured. Ask for a free pass for a complimentary ski day.

◆ If you lose a pole, stop by the rental desk and ask to borrow a new one. If you lose goggles or a mitten, drop by the lost and found and dig deep for one that's long-forgotten.

◆ If your equipment is stolen, ask for a free rental.

◆ If many lifts are closed due to winds or other natural occurrences, stop by the skier services desk and tell them your sad story of a botched vacation— and ask for a complimentary ticket.

◆ Most resorts do not charge lift ticket prices for young children. If you are introducing a child under five years old to the sport, ask if you can accompany them on the chair lift—free.

Special Report

More ski info available in the report "How to Get Anything You Want." Call 1-877-Pay-Nothing

Rent-a-Car Tricks

Speak Up!

Rental car counters are like Tootsie Roll Pops: work them long enough and you'll get to the sweet insides. But, if you bite down hard too early, you'll miss all the fun. Pay-Nothing Travelers routinely use a few, crucial tricks at the counter to get the most from this grab bag of treats.

◆ Ask for a Cell-phone: Tell the clerk about your concern for safety, and watch the free cell-phone roll out.

◆ Strap in the Child Seat: Budget normally offers no-charge child seats. If you choose another company, press the agent to match the deal. Chances are, the agent will buckle.

◆ You've Got Enough Insurance: Rental car agents typically get a commission on sales of the Collision Damage Waiver, which can double the cost of your rental. Chances are, you're already covered on your own automobile insurance policy. Check with your insurance agent before you rent to be sure.

Good idea

Give horrid details about your lousy day, and watch the big wheels roll out.

◆ Go For the Gold: The Hertz #1 Gold Club is a traveler's dream. AAA members get free enroll-ment—but paying the 50 bucks for membership is worth its tires. First, you're more likely to see the gold bus before you see the others, and that means less waiting and less fumes in your lungs. Second, you won't believe the service! Step on the bus and you feel like the King of Siam. They've got your name, your car spot, and zip-turn-zip, you arrive at a royal parking lot with your name in lights directing you to your car, which is never more than a few yards away. Then you drive off the lot while everyone else doesn't, and with a complimentary *USA Today* or *The Wall Street Journal* in hand.

24

◆ Pay Before Leaving the Country: Foreign rental agencies have been known to inflate prices, so pay stateside whenever possible.

◆ Get an Upgrade: Nobody goes to work wanting to do a bad job. Help the service agent reach service goals by nicely asking for an upgrade. Throw in details of your lousy day, and you could skip the econo-car and find yourself cruisin' in style.

◆ Don't Pick It Up at the Airport: Airport rental car companies charge an "airport concession fee," a rising, per-day cost somehow related to the company's parking garage deal at the airport. Don't pay it. You can save as much as 10% off your rental car bill by picking up your car at the nearest office—usually within distance of a cheap cab ride. Ask about the concession fee before you book your car.

Contact Information:

Budget
(800) 527-0700

Hertz
#1 Gold Club
(800) 654-3131

>see also: Pay-Nothing yellow pages, rental car companies

Don't Pay
For Broadway Tickets

Easy

Producers know that Broadway shows often represent special nights—nights on the town for most audiences—usually planned weeks in advance. That's why seats can easily approach $75 each, and Raisinettes sell at Pentagon prices. It's all about supply and demand, but the Pay-Nothing Traveler never falls for such voodoo economics.

Shows appearing in lesser towns than New York are especially easy to get into. Just call the manager of the local venue and offer up your services as an usher. With a little persistence, it's rarely a problem to get in. But getting into the big shows at favorable prices takes a bit of detective work.

♦ NYC's Theatre Development Fund is a theater appreciation group with cheap seats for loads of events and shows. An easy $14 and a quick membership application are all it takes. Another group, The Hit Show Club, distributes free coupons that get you substantial discounts off the box office price for Broadway's hottest shows.

> **Special Report**
>
> Call for the report "Pay Nothing for Super Bowl and Olympic Tickets." 1-877-Pay-Nothing

♦ BosTix, Boston's source for half-price tickets, starts selling at 11:00 a.m. throughout Beantown. A portion of the proceeds is used to support programs that introduce inner-city kids to the performing arts.

♦ TKTS is New York's source for half-price tickets, and they're located right in the center of Times Square (you can't miss it). Once the window opens, however, the line moves quickly; don't hold your breath for tickets to the hottest shows. Another, lesser-known location is in lower Manhattan at 2 World Trade Center.

Contact Information:
> see also: Pay-Nothing yellow pages, tickets

SAVE UP TO $100.00

Dining Clubs Worth Their Salt

Easy

Using dining club cards is like eating oysters: they're a lot more fun when no one's watching. That's why Pay-Nothing Travelers love programs such as Transmedia (below) for discreetly taking the meat right off the credit card invoice without having to show a cheesy card. Here are a few of our other favorites.

◆ In Good Taste (IGT): Check out their generous, free, six-month trial membership that shaves 25% off the tab at thousands of restaurants across the county. If you like it, it's $25 a year (and the small fee is refundable if the membership's cancelled).

◆ Premier Dining Card: Accepted at over 20,000 restaurants nationwide (with lots of two-for one offers), this card also earns discounts at participating movie theaters and fast food eateries. It costs just $49, including a free, three-month trial membership.

◆ Transmedia Card: For Pay-Nothing Travelers who dine at top-notch restaurants around the world, this card is the dining discount to claim. With more than 5,000 restaurants participating in the US, South America, Europe, and Australia, the Transmedia card consistently slices up to 20% off the bone for a measly $50 annual membership.

Secrets That Apply

• Join frequent customer programs!

Contact Information:

IGT Charge Card
(800) 444-8872

Premier Dining Card
(800) 346-3241

Transmedia Card
(800) 422-5090

SAVE UP TO $100.00

Sleep in a Dorm

When summer arrives, college students will flee campuses like rats from sinking ships. Empty schools mean vacant dorms and cheap rooms for Pay-Nothing Travelers seeking to one-up the hostels and avoid the hotels. Oftentimes, campuses are located in beautiful and centrally located spots. The Campus Lodging Guide gives phone numbers for dorms and lodges throughout the US.

Contact Information:

The Campus Lodging Guide, B&J Publications PO Box 5486 Fullerton, CA 92635 (800) 525-6633

>see also: Pay-Nothing yellow pages, lodging—college

SAVE UP TO $100.00

Tip Before You Receive

Speak Up!

T ipping after the service is like paying the guy at the Whack-a-Mole stand: he'll gladly take your money, but you're not going home with any prizes. Pay-Nothing Travelers, on the other hand, want it all. That's why they employ skilled tipping (called "greasing" in lesser circles), and grab the goods while holding on to their tokens.

As a rule, people in the front lines of service—and those best positioned to help—are underpaid. By all means, approach them first. That means doormen, bouncers, maitre d's, ushers, and hotel clerks, to name just a few. Just let the front lines know you appreciate their power, and compensate them for it. Here are a few ideas to get you to the front row:

♦ Tip the maitre d' 50% of the price of one person's meal to gain quick access to the best table.

♦ Tip the bursar at least $100 per person to upgrade your cabin. The bursar is your go-to guy: the better the tip, the better the upgrade.

♦ Tip doormen about $20 to gain access to clubs and avoid those long lines and expensive cover charges.

♦ Tip ushers $10 to upgrade your seat.

♦ Tip the hotel desk clerk 20% of the price of a room for a champion upgrade.

♦ Tip the concierge $5 for finding a babysitter, $10 for discount theme park tickets, and $20 for getting you seats to professional sporting events.

Great Tip

Carefully fold the bill in the palm of your hand and offer your new friend a brief glimpse.

Contact Information:
>see also: Pay-Nothing yellow pages, tipping

Upgrade Your Tour of Washington, DC For Nada

W ith more art on display than a first grader's refrigerator exhibit, the museums of Washington, DC are a Paris meets Egypt collection of incredible salutes to our nation's progress. But with millions of visitors rubbernecking together, it's a little like watching a movie on a moving platform. Pay-Nothing Travelers cut through the crowd and opt for a call to the Capitol. This quick call will score them contact information for their state Senator or Congressional Representative.

These elected officials receive blocks of tickets to some of DC's hottest sites, and they're always available to you and your family. Here are a few of the tours you can receive:

Good idea
• Whenever possible, take the train into centrally located Union Station.

◆ A special, guided tour of White House (even while the President is home).

◆ Gallery passes to see both houses of the Congress in session (so you can watch your tax dollars being spent by the billions).

◆ Guided tours of the Capitol.

◆ Tours of FBI offices and facilities (where you can see an exhibit of infamous weapons of assassination).

◆ Tours of the Holocaust Museum.

Most DC hot spots are free, of course, including the Smithsonian Institute Museums, the National Galleries, and our national monuments, including the Tomb of the Unknown Soldier, the Vietnam War Memorial, and Arlington National Cemetery.

Contact Information:
The US Capitol Building (202) 225-3121

SAVE UP TO $100.00

Find a Room in a Fully Booked Town

Speak Up!

Hotel rooms get put on Most Wanted lists whenever a massive convention comes to town. The same goes for a popular concert in a small town. So, if you find yourself arriving in a small town during a surprise Garth Brooks concert, here's how to navigate the jungle—Pay-Nothing style.

◆ Ask for a parlor room. These hotel rooms are normally reserved for meetings. They're regular rooms without beds. Call in a cot, and insist on a half-priced rate.

◆ Ask about "Presidential" or "Governor" suites. These rooms are high-ticket, so they're not offered to just anyone who walks through the door. If you're told a hotel's booked, just plunk your credit card on the counter and ask about the suites—any suite. Once you're offered the suite, refer to the tactics on page 61 to deep six the room rate.

Secrets That Apply
- Be a travel writer!
- Be "on business!"
- Complain!

◆ Call the Chamber of Commerce. Look them up in the phone book and make your problem their problem. They'll find you a cancellation or arrange for board at a local home.

◆ Call a Local College. With dorm rooms empty in the summer and between semesters, many colleges will rent dorm rooms at super cheap rates. Clean and cheap, this is a diamond in the rough.

◆ Call Your Fraternity or Sorority Chapter. If you were in a fraternity, or know someone who was, contact the local chapter and ask for help.

Contact Information:

>see also: Pay-Nothing yellow pages, lodging—hotels, colleges

Free Admission to Popular Museums

The Pay-Nothing Traveler can view some of the world's greatest art and oddities without paying admission. Most big-city museums, and even some hometown galleries, have at least one evening each month when people can steal a peek at their hallowed halls—without getting robbed.

◆ Boston: The Boston Museum of Fine Arts opens its doors for free on Wednesday nights. Harvard museums pony up every Saturday morning from 10:00 a.m. 'til noon. The Institute of Contemporary Art won't charge you Thursday nights from 5:00 to 9:00 p.m.; and the first Friday night of each month is free at the Peabody Essex Museum.

◆ Chicago: The newly re-opened Chicago Museum of Contemporary Art now opens its doors with free admission on the first Tuesday of each month.

◆ San Francisco: The Museum of Modern Art, known as MOMA to the locals, is free on the first Tuesday of every month, and admission is only half price every Thursday night.

◆ Seattle visitors can enjoy the Seattle Museum of Art for free on the first Thursday of each month, and Seniors Pay Nada on Fridays.

Even if you haven't seen any free museum admission advertised in your area, call around to get the inside track. Case in point: Atlanta's High Museum. It opens for free on the first Saturday of every month, but only for Fulton County residents. Even if a museum does charge an admission fee, it's usually on the pay-what-you-can scale; the fee is really just a suggested donation.

Contact Information:

>see also: Pay-Nothing yellow pages, museums

32

Intermission
is the Ticket

E vents such as Broadway shows and professional sports games always begin with a frenzied crowd rushing to catch the first act or foul ball. It's enough to win a scalpers heart. If you ever find yourself in a city that's hosting an event you weren't planning to see, why not play the spontaneous card and catch a great second act or 60 minutes of live, professional sports? Neither will cost the Pay-Nothing Traveler a dime. Just slip in during intermission.

This trick is best to try on events that you're not otherwise planning to see. For instance, a Broadway show low on your list or a sports team playing against some visiting Joes. In most cases, the doors swing wide open during intermission, halftime, or the seventh inning stretch. Still, it's a good idea to find and tip an usher who might suggest an open seat.

Good Idea

• Tip the usher!

Free
Vacation Videos

Before you spend big bucks to end up laying out in a landfill, consider previewing your destination by video. There are several ways a Pay-Nothing Traveler can get these goods.

First, check with your travel agent to see if he/she can loan you some promo tapes for a few days. Two companies that specialize in vacation videos include International Video Network and Mentor Productions. Blockbuster Video maintains a "Special Interest" section of their own with tourism videos representing all corners of the world. While some of the videos are free, some can carry a $2 or $3 rental fee, which varies according to store location.

Secrets That Apply

- Learn travel agent skills!

Contact Information:

International Video Network
(800) 669-4486

Mentor Productions
(800) 521-5104

Blockbuster Video <www.blockbuster.com>

SAVE UP TO $100.00

Around the World for $10 a Night

Growing up and leaving home is the American way. Now, think of the millions of vacant rooms left behind. Rooms with views. Luxury rooms; simple rooms. Now think about those empty rooms all over the world. From New England to New Zealand, there's a place for the Pay-Nothing Traveler. If you're over 50 years old, the Evergreen Bed & Breakfast Club is for you.

The Evergreen Bed & Breakfast Club is a first-class option for traveling seniors. For about 10 bucks a night, you can stay over in a club member's home in any of a thousand destinations throughout the US and around the world. Plus, breakfast is usually a given. How do you like your eggs?

Secrets That Apply
• Travel write!
• Be "on business"
• Volunteer!

Contact Information:

The Evergreen Bed & Breakfast Club
PO Box 1430
Falls Church, VA 22041
(800) 962-2392

SAVE UP TO $100.00

35

Get Around Excess Baggage Charges

It's a rite of passage to bring too much stuff on vacation. That's why domestic Pay-Nothing Travelers plan wisely to avoid the $50 per-extra-bag fine at the airport counter. They ship their bulky duds directly to the destination.

If you can ship your extra luggage a couple days before leaving, United Parcel Service is your best option. An average suitcase shipment going from New York City to Chicago will cost about 12 bucks. If you're planning a multi-activity trip, such as beaches and sightseeing, you may wish to ship towels and beach chairs via a carrier such as Greyhound. The old, doggie-bus company goes everywhere, and their rates are kibble.

Contact Information:

United Parcel Service
(800) 742-5877

Greyhound Package Express
(800) 739-5020

SAVE UP TO $100.00

Free
Breakfast in Bed

Speak Up!

T ravel agents are under the gun to provide value. Though their services are free to the public, a price is ultimately paid by the consumer. Travelers who use an agent can choose to turn a cheek to the agent's final number. Pay-Nothing Travelers, however, never comply without squeezing the agent for costly extras before uttering their credit card number.

Here are a few items any good travel agent will provide for no additional cost: room service, bottles of wine, free transfers, fruit baskets, flowers, and in-room movies. Ask and you shall receive.

Secrets That Apply

• Insist on the upgrade!

Contact Information:

The American Society of Travel Agents (ASTA)
(703) 739-2782

Camp Anywhere for Free

Free

Camping season can bring Pay-Nothing Travelers tire-to-tire with converted mini-vans and flickering televisions. *Speak Up!* It's getting harder to avoid the crowds in the places you want to be, so here are our best tips.

◆ National Forests: Over 461 million acres of prime American land are managed by the National Forest Service (NFS) and the Bureau of Land Management (BLM). Pay-Nothing Travelers seeking private, pristine campsites for rest and recreation point their collective compasses toward these mostly free, natural gems. Just plant your gear at least a quarter mile away from any trailhead, campground, or shelter, and you're in for free. Be sure to check with the NFS for rules pertaining to specific parks and trails.

◆ Public Parks: When you're passing through a small town, ask the local police if you can pitch a tent in the village green, park, or even a schoolyard on weekends. The key to success here is specific language and how you look. First, it's better to have other people with you, and kids are the real gold mine. It's not likely that a lone male will pull this off, so gather your buds—particularly the females. Second, using phrases like "no fires" and "clean camping" usually win the nod.

◆ Private Homes: Stop by the local health food store, camping supply store, or bicycle shop. Just walk in and ask the hired help if they know of a great place where some adventurers could pitch tents for free, with no fires. This should yield several locations, and maybe even invites to prime, local campsites. If, however, you run out of luck, don't overlook basic human kindness. If you spot a large farm or clear lot, stop by the nearest house and knock on the door. Remember to stand away from the door, and drag the kids to the porch if you've got 'em. Explain what you're doing and ask if you could camp on that site (and point at it) until 8:00 a.m., and no fires. Not only will you likely land your campsite, you could even pick up a free meal or cookout.

Contact Information:
National Forest Service & Bureau of Land Mngt.
<www.recreation.gov>

38

Free Emergency Health Advice

N othing will terrify a Pay-Nothing Traveler more than contracting an exotic virus while lounging on the Gulf Coast of Florida or volcanic beaches of Maui. For that reason, Ask-a-Nurse operates a toll-free phone service that provides quick, free access to basic health advice. In addition, Ask-a-Nurse will direct you to the nearest hospital for treatment.

Another great service is provided by the People's Medical Society. They publish a handy booklet called "Dial 800 for Health." For a cheap $10.95, Pay-Nothing Travelers can find hundreds of toll-free numbers for health-related services and organizations.

Even if you're not globe-trotting, there's nothing more distressing than being the host of a botulism-infested barbecue. That's why the US Department of Agriculture set up a toll-free number to provide tips and advice on food safety. Before dipping into that sun-baked chicken casserole, you may want to give them a call.

Contact Information:

Ask-a-Nurse
(800) 535-1111
People's Medical Society
(800) 624-8773
Department of Agriculture
(800) 535-4555
>see also: Pay-Nothing yellow pages, medical assistance

Free Limo Service

Speak Up! Free

Y ou probably know that many hotels offer free downtown shuttle service to and from the airport; Pay-Nothing Travelers use these free rides to maximum advantage. Before you chunk out the change for a rental car or taxi from the airport to any downtown destinations, call a hotel in your destination area, and ask if you can take the shuttle. After checking out their property for a possible overnight stay, stroll down to where you need to be. It's never a problem.

Many hotel shuttle services will even take you around town, picking you up and dropping you off on command. A great example is the Radisson Hotel in Midtown Los Angeles, offering free shuttle service anywhere you want to go in downtown LA within a five-mile radius of the hotel.

Hotels that are just on the perimeter of tourist destinations and cities normally provide free shuttle service to keep guests smiling. If you're in a bind, a well-placed tip to anyone resembling a parking attendant will always get you where you need to go. For our money, it sure beats expensive rental cars or taxis with pricey ride zones.

Secrets That Apply

- Travel write!
- Be "on business"
- Travel agent skills!
- Frequent customer programs!
- Tip the driver!

Contact Information:

>see also: Pay-Nothing yellow pages, limousine service and lodging

SAVE UP TO $100.00

Get Free Gold

Easy Free

There are a few vacation spots where an adventurous prospector can still take a shot at gold mining. One popular place is Dahlonega, Georgia, the site of the first US gold rush. Here, lucky families are still finding gold and gems in their pans. Keep your day job, though; most of the big stuff's been gone since 1828. For more information on gold and how to find it, contact the US government's listing on this page and request their free information.

While you're at it, ask for other free brochures on subjects such as rock collecting, dinosaurs, earthquakes, and maps and compasses. They even have some cool posters for kids, as well as information packets ideal for teachers interested in teaching geology-related topics.

Contact Information:

The Dahlonega, Georgia
Welcome Center
(706) 864-3711

US Geological Survey
Information Services
(800) 435-7627

>see also: Pay-Nothing
yellow pages, government

Contact Information:

The American Society
of Travel Agents (ASTA)
(703) 739-2782

Ask-a-Nurse
(800) 535-1111

Blockbuster Video
<www.blockbuster.com>

Budget
(800) 527-0700

The Campus Lodging Guide
B&J Publications
PO Box 5486
Fullerton, CA 92635
(800) 525-6633

The Dahlonega, Georgia
Welcome Center
(706) 864-3711

The Evergreen Bed
& Breakfast Club
PO Box 1430
Falls Church, VA 22041
(800) 962-2392

Greyhound Package Express
(800) 739-5020

Hertz
#1 Gold Club
(800) 654-3131

IGT Charge Card
(800) 444-8872

International Video Network
(800) 669-4486

National Forest Service &
Bureau of Land Mngt.
<www.recreation.gov>

People's Medical Society (800)
624-8773

Premier Dining Card
(800) 346-3241

Mentor Productions
(800) 521-5104

Transmedia Card
(800) 422-5090

United Parcel Service
(800) 742-5877

The US Capitol Building
(202) 225-3121

US Department
of Agriculture
(800) 535-4555

US Geological Survey
Information Services
(800) 435-7627

Chapter 3

Save up to $1000.00

Turn Coach into First Class

Speak Up!

H owever good or bad your flight is, it's always better in first class. Trouble is, the additional cost looks worse than the lavatory of a New York to Tokyo flight. So, fuh-get-a-bout-it! Let the common man ride in the rear, and follow the hobbling Pay-Nothing Traveler feigning their way to the front car.

First, make note of any empty seats in first class. Next, think of a reason why you are so deserving. Having an extremely sore injury or a sudden case of claustrophobia are two winning ailments. If you have more work to do than pro boxing leagues but the kid behind you is practicing low blows on your seat-back, ask the ref for a TKO to first class. This decision is entirely at the will of the attendant, so be nice.

Special Report

Call for the report "Low Cost Airlines: Full Disclosure." 1-877-Pay-Nothing

Talk Up
the Occasion

Speak Up!

Repeat business means everything in the hospitality industry. Most quality organizations, including restaurants, hotels, water-sport centers, and theme parks, build their entire marketing plans around getting visitors to come back. For instance, most of these companies snuggle up to honeymooners hoping for decades of dollars. Wise Pay-Nothing Travelers understand this shmoozing and exploit it.

Tell a service provider that you're on your honeymoon and prices will drop faster than a garter belt in a hall full of bachelors. The same goes for an anniversary. But did you know that birthdays, celebrations, and even multiple visits ("we come here whenever we're in town") will likely do the same? Work these angles hard, and you'll either see a tiny bill or witness Imelda-like gifts shoeing their way to your door or table.

Don't wait a moment to spread the good news. When making a reservation, however short or long, mention the occasion and instruct the telephone clerk to pass the message on to management. When you arrive, watch the goods roll out. If no reservations were made, sing your song to everyone you see. Finally, consider destinations that cater to honeymooners—such as any place in Hawaii or the Pocono Mountains in Pennsylvania.

Contact Information:
>see also: Pay-Nothing yellow pages, lodging—hotels, resorts—Hawaii, Poconos

SAVE UP TO $1,000.00

Get a Second Hotel Room For 50% Off

Speak Up!

Companion rooms (also called nanny rooms) are set aside for families with a couple of kids, a nanny, or accompanying guests. After hearing the thud of their initial room-rate hitting rock bottom (page 61), Pay-Nothing Travelers turn to chiseling out a cheap space for their creations. Here's the best of the hotel bunch:

◆ Hyatt Hotels: If you book a room at a Hyatt Resort, you can get a second room for your kids or additional guests for 50% off. The availability of these rooms is limited, so be sure to check with the hotel before making reservations.

◆ Hilton Hotels: Hilton limits the companion room program to its foreign resorts. If you stay at a Hilton hotel outside the US, you can get a companion room for 50% off.

◆ Radisson Hotels: Radisson sets aside a few companion rooms each day and chops 25% off the rate.

◆ Holiday Inn: Holiday Inn does not have corporate provisions for companion rooms. At individual hotels, however, we were able to talk down a couple of solid discounts off second rooms.

◆ Ritz-Carlton: Book the "Junior Presidential Suite" for your kids and make sure the connecting door closes. That's because this special room is filled with toys, kid-sized furniture, bathroom fixtures, and a mini-fridge stocked with your darling's favorite snacks. Prices vary, but you will likely save 20% off the cost of the second room.

Contact Information:

Hyatt Hotels	(800) 233-1234
Hilton Hotels	(800) 445-8667
Radisson Hotels	(800) 333-3333
Holiday Inn	(800) 465-4329
Ritz-Carlton	(800) 241-3333

SAVE UP TO $1,000.00

Pretend You're 62 Years Old

Easy

I f you're 62 years or older, a world of double-digit discounts awaits you. If you're not, the Pay-Nothing Traveler would be wise to get a fake ID. Check out these programs:

◆ Continental Airlines: For a pension-friendly $579, those age 62 and over have rights to a book of four one-way tickets good for destinations in the 48 contiguous states, Mexico, Canada, and the Caribbean. An eight-ticket booklet is also available for $1,079. Also, The Freedom Flight Club ($75) offers 15-20% off any fare Continental offers.

◆ American Airlines: Travelers age 62 and above are eligible to receive four, one-way tickets to anywhere American flies, including overseas, for $596. Some blackout dates apply, so be sure to check carefully.

◆ Delta Airlines: The love-to-fly people's "Young at Heart" program offers a globe-trotting coupon program good for four one-way tickets to anywhere Delta flies for $596. Restrictions apply, so give them a call.

◆ America West Airlines: "Senior Savers" is a program that'll land seniors four one-way vouchers for $548. A great transferable policy allows two of the vouchers to be used by grandchildren ages two through 12—when accompanied by a traveling program member.

Contact Information:

Continental Airlines
(800) 441-1135

Delta Airlines
(800) 221-1212

American Airlines
(800) 237-7981

American West Airlines
(800) 235-9292

SAVE UP TO $1,000.00

Cheap World Travel for Students and Educators

Easy

$\mathbf{I}$f you're a student or teacher who moonlights as a Pay-Nothing Traveler, you're eligible for a special card from Council Travel, a division of the Council on International Educational Exchange (CIEE). The CIEE was founded 52 years ago to promote student and educator exchange around the world. For only 20 bucks, overseas travelers will love this card's ability to turn deutsche marks into dust everywhere from the airport to hotels to rental cars.

◆ EuroRail Pass: The card allows purchase of a 10-day train pass throughout Western Europe for about $65 a day.

◆ Discounts: We cried when we had to finally put away our student ID's and get real jobs. We remember how they could win favor in all sorts of places, and the CIEE card is no different. Museums and theme parks around the world honor this friend. You can even contact Council Travel to slice the price on airfares and hotels from the US to Holland to Thailand. When calling the 800 number below, be sure to ask for the number of the Council Travel office nearest you.

Great Tip

• *Travel write!*

Contact Information:

CIEE: 205 E. 42nd Street, New York, NY 10017
(888) 268-6245

Council Travel
(800) 2-COUNCIL (226-8624)

SAVE UP TO $1,000.00

51

Best Clicks

Easy

I f all of us are ever permanently banned from the Internet, we'll bet that travel agents are behind the scam. The Internet continues to supply the Pay-Nothing Traveler with all he/she needs, but following these specific clicks will get you there faster.

◆ Online Booking: Check flight schedules, ticket prices, and book your flights directly with the air carrier. It's easy, it's dependable, and it works. Tickets are usually sent to your home, but some last-minute deals can require you to pick them up at the airport or boarding dock.

◆ Matching Services: Services such as Priceline.com allow you to bid on empty seats. Many of these services have cumbersome entry processes and lousy restrictions, but they can save wads of cash.

When a deal looks like it matches your vacation plans, they'll send you an e-mail, and you can book the trip directly over the Internet.

Air Carriers

America Airlines	\<www.AA.com\>
Continental Airlines	\<www.continental.com\>
Delta Airlines	\<www.Delta-air.com\>
United Airlines	\<www.ual.com\>
US Airways	\<www.usairways.com\>

Online Booking Companies

Priceline	\<www.priceline.com\>
Cheaptickets	\<www.cheaptickets.com\>
Bestfares	\<www.Bestfares.com\>
1travel	\<www.1travel.com\>
Expedia	\<www.expedia.com\>
Travelcity	\<www.travelcity.com\>
Frequentfliers	\<www.frequentfliers.com\>

52

Vacation at Recovering Resorts

Smokin!

W̅hen hurricane season hits the tropics, resorts shutter. That's because the press emphasizes each disaster as a national event, scaring the Bermuda shorts off everyone even considering a visit. Needless to say, a hurricane may ravage one section of town while leaving another virtually unscathed. That's where Pay-Nothing Travelers see savings in the sea spray. Be savvy— after a quick call to the State Department, you can be lounging half-price in resorts you might never afford otherwise. Here's how to find the gems through the wreckage.

◆ Consider traveling during storm season: The National Hurricane Center/Tropical Prediction Center in Miami, Florida is America's resource for hurricane and tropical storm information. Tropical storm systems can be tracked from their website. They're so good at predicting storms, they've figured out that September 9 is the day the East Coast will most likely be hit by a hurricane. While the Atlantic hurricane season runs from June 1 to November 30, most storms occur between August 20 and October 10.

◆ Call the Area Tourist Association as soon as the clouds pass. Tourist areas are so eager for post-storm business, that local merchants rain discounts on anyone even posing as a tourist. For instance, following a major decrease in tourism after Hurricane Hugo, local hotels in St. Croix offered a free rental car to anyone staying longer than five days.

Secrets That Apply
• Travel write!
• Upgrade!
• Be a travel agent!

Here are a few hurricane hits over the past several years:

◆ Honduras: Hurricane Mitch, the country's worst in 200 years, made landfall on March 12, 1999. Many of the nation's resorts are still rebuilding.

Continued ➡

Smokin!

♦ Five of the top 10 most powerful Atlantic hurricanes of the 20th century have occurred within the past decade. As these deadly storms increase, so do the number of resorts that lie in their path. Hurricanes Andrew (August, 1992) and Hugo (September, 1989) both wailed this very corridor.

Contact Information:

The National Hurricane Center/Tropical Prediction Center
(305) 227-4470
<www.nhc.noaa.gov>

The State Department

SAVE UP TO $1,000.00

Financial Aid
for the Older & Wiser

If you consider yourself well traveled, you might be looking for new excitement when you hit the road. Educational tours don't always have to involve busses and microphones. Pay-Nothing Travelers seeking to sharpen their IQs might consider this incredible program of learning and adventure.

Elderhostel, a non-profit organization committed to being the preeminent provider of high quality, affordable, educational opportunities for older adults, blends travel and on-campus education throughout the US, Great Britain, and Ireland. The network utilizes local university dorms and participating organizations to integrate seniors into learning environments. While most of the programs require that you travel on your own to the site, the organization offers a few, all-inclusive scholarly packages in beautiful and luxurious settings.

Contact Information:

Elderhostel
(877) 426-8056
<www.elderhostel.org>

SAVE UP TO $1,000.00

Free PGA Tickets

Smokin!

Buying tickets for ultra-hot events like PGA Tournaments often requires your consent to medical experiments—and mega-cash. But the Pay-Nothing Traveler avoids the evil scalpers and doctors up a new plan.

The PGA hosts over 120 big-name tournaments each year. The Tour, as well as the individual courses that hold these events, are always on the prowl for volunteers to herd crowds, administer first aid, translate or interpret languages, or host visiting dignitaries. Your good deed will be rewarded with heavily discounted or free passes to the fairways. An interesting catch should be noted: you are required to buy the official jersey for each tournament you participate in—not a bad souvenir.

Special Report "Pay Nothing for Super Bowl and Olympic Tickets." 1-877-Pay-Nothing

The LPGA established its own division of volunteers to assist with their busy tour schedule. The guidelines surrounding LPGA volunteers differ slightly from PGA volunteer guidelines, depending on the tour location. Be sure to contact them for the latest tour information and volunteer needs.

Contact Information:

The PGA (904) 285-3700 <http://pgatour.com>
The LPGA (904) 274-6200 <www.lpga.com>

SAVE UP TO $1,000.00

Free Cross-Continental Road Trips

Free

Easy

Pay-Nothing Travelers on the one-way ticket plan will likely enjoy delivering a car to a distant state, or even Canada. The reputable Auto Driveaway Company hires travelers to drive other people's cars to and from over 75 destination cities throughout the US and Canada. All you need is cash for gas and a general plan. Taking friends isn't a problem, either.

The company requires all drivers to be 21 or older, and to pony up a $250-350 refundable deposit. But if you think about it, it's not the pickup truck crowd who generally want their cars chauffeured to a distant state. It's more like Madame Muffy and her Mercedes convertible.

Secrets That Apply
- Travel write!
- Travel "on business!"
- Volunteer!

Contact Information:

Auto Driveaway Company
310 South Michigan Avenue
Chicago, IL 60604
(800) 346-2277

Fly Through
Family Emergencies

Speak Up!

Smokin!

Τ he last thing the Pay-Nothing Traveler needs to deal with during a family emergency is a whopping airfare bill. Last-minute travel can confound even our most frugal editor. Sure, bereavement fares get you to the funeral home in a hurry, and often for 50% off the last-minute fare, but everyone knows that. The "compassion" fares a few airlines offer are the real secret.

Compassion fares are for people who need to visit hospitalized or home-care family members who aren't necessarily on their last legs. These offers change regularly, and you need to specifically ask for them in order to receive the offer. You should also be prepared to show documentation (the name and phone number of the attending physician and/or the name and number for the hospital) at the time of purchase. We found Continental to be one of the most compassionate, offering 50% off coach fare for those traveling to visit a family member in the hospital.

Secrets That Apply
- Airline industry expert
- Complain!

Contact Information:
>see also: Pay-Nothing yellow pages, airlines and travel agencies

SAVE UP TO $1,000.00

Love an Airline Coupon Broker

Easy

Coupon brokers are matchmakers. They unite air travelers who want to sell discounted or frequent flyer miles with travelers who want to buy them. One important note: purchasing a brokered ticket is against airline rules, but it's not illegal. Airlines are well within their rights to leave you at the airport if they discover your brokered ticket. But don't worry too much: this almost never happens.

There are two ways to save huge using a coupon broker. First, they can trim the fat off any business class fare you are quoted. Second, they're the absolute cheapest ticket for last minute travel. For example, a round trip, first class flight from the East Coast to Australia might normally cost a lottery-winning $7,000-8,000 during peak season. A coupon broker can typically get you that same round trip seat for 60% less.

In general, the more expensive the ticket, the bigger the savings coupon brokers can offer you. And remember, the coupons are usually good for a year, and you can make any changes to your travel date without paying penalties.

Special Report

Call for the report "Low Cost Airlines: Full Disclosure."
1-877-Pay-Nothing

Contact Information:

International Air Coupon Exchange
(800) 558-0053

SAVE UP TO $1,000.00

Use a Hotel Consolidator—Free

Most hotels are usually only 60-70% full, or 30-40% empty, depending upon how the Pay-Nothing Traveler looks at things. Whichever way you look, room rates routinely drop at the last minute as clerks scurry to fill rooms. To properly exploit this unfortunate situation, big city discount services are the place to call.

Operating somewhat like airline consolidators (see page 52), these services offer rooms at mondo savings—up to 65%—when hotels are anticipating vast vacancies. The list on this page is a selection of some of the best services. These services are absolutely free. Just be ready to give your credit card number for a deposit at the time of booking, and show your card or coupon when you check in.

Secrets That Apply
• Travel write!
• Be "on business"
• Upgrade!
• Complain!
• Be a travel agent!
• Frequent customer!

Contact Information:

Accommodations Express (800) 444-7666; California Reservations (800) 576-0003; Hotel Plus (800) 235-0909; Hotel Reservations Network (800) 964-6835; The Room Exchange (800) 846-7000

SAVE UP TO $1,000.00

Declare War
on Hotel Prices

Speak Up!

T he Pay-Nothing Traveler is a master negotiator when telephoning central reservations and a fast talker at the front desk. These skills pay off big: forcing the hotel to smack down its rates while upping the quality of service.

◆ Central Reservations: It's best to call central reservations when you're planning a trip several weeks in advance. Never accept the first price they give you, known as the rack rate. Negotiate that rate down 10-65% by naming any organizations you belong to, including AAA or any other travel clubs. If you're booking for a weekend, ask the clerk for the corporate rate and watch your savings get promoted.

Special Report

Call for the step-by-step guide "Slash Hotel Rates Worldwide!"
1-877-Pay-Nothing

◆ Contact the Hotel Directly: If your target stay-date is coming up within a week, the best rate will be found by calling the hotel directly. Have the central reservations best rate already researched, then tell the front desk clerk at your specific hotel that it's way north of your budget. Next, throw out a new number, be specific, and go low. If you don't get lucky and land that rate, chances are good the clerk will give you whatever really is the lowest possible rate.

◆ Day of Stay: Down to the last minute? It's best to call the hotel directly, but after 6:00 p.m., when most of the reservations have already been made. Your goal is to take advantage of the hotel's hopefully low occupancy rate (often 60-70%). Then, force them to give up a room at your budget—or at up to 50% off the rack rate. If that doesn't work—or if the hotel is fully booked—ask for a parlor room. These are fully functional rooms that require a cot and are very rarely used.

Beat the Airlines

Easy

When booking tickets without the assistance of a travel agent, Pay-Nothing Travelers employ several effective, legal ways of dropping the drawers on high-ticket prices. And remember, whenever you book, avoid e-tickets and opt for the actual paper tickets—you'll need them. The following schemes are legal in the US, but not encouraged by the airlines.

◆ Back-to-back ticketing

With a seven to 14 day advance, purchasing two roundtrip tickets (one roundtrip ticket to your destination, one roundtrip from your destination) is far cheaper than buying one mid-week trip. Coordinate the dates well, and you will have bought two tickets for typically 50-75% of the cost of the one mid-week travel ticket.

◆ Hidden City Fares

Airlines often run specials to certain destinations that include stopovers in "hidden" cities. If the city you want to get to is one of the hidden cities, you might be able to save big bucks on an otherwise expensive airfare. Check the hub cities at the end of this section, and choose the airline that is likely to go through your hidden city destination.

Special Report
Call for the comprehensive guide "Low-cost Airlines: Full Disclosure."
Call 1-877-Pay-Nothing

62

◆ Reverse Hidden City Fares

Flights take off from an origin city. Find out how much you can save by booking the ticket from this origin city to your final destination by calling the airlines and airports. Then jump on board in the city most convenient.

◆ Hub Cities

TWA:	New York
Delta:	Cincinnati, Atlanta
Continental:	Houston, Cleveland, Newark
USAir:	Pittsburgh, Philadelphia, Washington, DC, Charlotte
American:	Chicago

Secrets That Apply
• Travel "on business!"
• Be an airline expert!
• Be a travel agent!

Contact Information:

>see also: Pay-Nothing yellow pages, airlines

Free Luxury
Rooms in Vermont

Pay-Nothing Travelers can visit historic Stowe, Vermont in late April and stay in any number of hotels, bed & breakfasts, and resorts for zilch.

Here's how it works: around the time of Mother's Day, you and the family can crash for no cash. By offering free lodging, the Stowe Area Association hopes to promote more guest shopping with the local merchants. The merchants, in turn, selflessly donate their proceeds toward breast cancer research. The free rooms are available for only one day, and this program is incredibly popular—keep posted. While staying-on-the house, Pay-Nothing Travelers can enjoy spectacular scenery, as well as hiking, bicycling, antique-ing, and over 50 restaurants.

Contact Information

The Stowe Area Association
(802) 253-7321
<www.gostowe.com>

64

SAVE UP TO $1,000.00

Eat Free
in Restaurants

Smokin! Free

F ine restaurants are obsessed with customer feedback, and organizations exist that test and critique everything from bread rolls to after-dinner mints. Somewhere in between lies the Pay-Nothing Traveler who skillfully volunteers their taste buds for the good of mankind—and a free meal.

The PayNada.com Editors continue to be astounded at the availability of "sampling" jobs—called "secret shopping" in marketing circles. Bare Associates International is a major employer of secret shoppers and evaluators for all types of businesses. Shop and Check runs a similar service for retail stores, restaurants, and fast food joints. Before you start chewing, both companies have brief application processes for you to complete. Also, they require that you write brief reports on your experiences.

Secrets That Apply
- Volunteer!
- Complain!

Follow some simple guidelines, and you can be critiquing restaurants, bars, health clubs and even hotels all over the country—and on someone else's tab. What's more, you may even be paid for each report you write.

Contact Information:

Bare Associates International
(800) 296-6699 <www.rhscorp.com>

Shop and Check, PO Box 740045, Atlanta, GA 30374
(800) 669-6526 <www.shopncheck.com>

Don't Get Mad, Get Comped

Speak Up! Easy

Companies such as airlines, rental car agencies, hotels, restaurants, and even manufacturers care more about your complaints than Mom. Pay-Nothing Travelers know that front-line personnel are instructed to hand out the freebies to customers in distress. That's why they use the complaint box to their advantage—and walk away that much richer. Need practice? Call your credit card company and tell the representative that your rate is too high, especially compared to another company's offer. They'll drop it on the spot. Here lies a crash course in skilled complaining:

◆ Look for Stuff: Be aware of services that are not to your liking, and take them to the service counter.

◆ Be Nice: They'll appreciate your patience and are more apt to shower you with gifts.

◆ Explain, explain, explain: Tell them the problem in great detail. Emphasize that you are a frequent customer.

Special Report

Call for your copy of "One Year Past Warranty? No Problem!" Call 1-877-Pay-Nothing

◆ Offer Suggestions: Have an idea about how the establishment can correct the problem, and always think big. Ten percent off is an absolute minimum you should receive, and always try to obtain the make-good certificate on the spot.

SAVE UP TO $1,000.00

Enjoy America's Cities Without Paying

Easy

Smokin!

$\mathbf{I}$f your relationship with coupons has never gone past two-for-one Ovaltine, it's time to stir up your chocolate milk. We're not suggesting you ruin your Sunday with a pair of scissors and a stack of circulars; find five bucks and turn it into the best coupon ever made available to the Pay-Nothing Traveler.

Cash Savers, a promotional group, has announced two-night stays in Las Vegas for the purchase of a $4.00 coupon. What's more, the offer is now available in many other, major American cities. In Vegas alone, that $4 gift certificate is good for three days' and two nights' stay at a luxurious hotel. If there is a catch, we haven't found it, so pack your bags and read on.

That $4 gift certificate will also score you $500 worth of casino benefits good for gaming, food, and drinks at various casinos around town. In addition to the measly $4, you'll just have to pay room tax (approximately $8 or less per night). The only restrictions are that you are 21 or older, the reservations are booked midweek, and you haven't used this killer offer in the last year.

Hang on to your bottle of sun block, because there are 19 other incredible cities for you to visit. Cash Saver offers travelers similar programs in unique places such as the Hacienda Buena Ventura in Puerto Vallarta, a first-class, waterfront resort where it can cost the Pay-Nothing Traveler a mere $18 a night to vacation in style. It's a good idea to check with Cash Savers before booking your flight, so be sure to give them a call.

Contact Information:

Cash Saver
(888) 327-8971 or (702) 642-5556
<www.lasvegascomps.com/LasVegas.htm>

SAVE UP TO $1,000.00

Ski Across the USA for Free

Easy *Free*

T he Pay-Nothing Traveler knows that the real color of gold is white. That's because when the snow falls—or even when it doesn't—overbuilt ski resorts drop prices faster than bartenders at happy hour.

♦ **In the west:** Crested Butte, Colorado tops our list for best invitation. This world class resort, renowned for some of the country's best black diamond trails, sponsors "Ski Free Days" for a few weeks each year. That means the $49 lift ticket is waived during these days, saving a family of four a bundle of dough. During the '98-'99 season, "Ski Free Days" ran from November 20 to December 19 and again from April 5-18, but call ahead to make sure. When they're not skiing free, kids under 12 pay their age for a great ticket. Here are a few other great ski ideas:

Secrets That Apply
- *Travel write!*
- *Be a travel agent!*
- *Be an expert!*
- *Frequent customer!*

♦ **In Colorado and New Hampshire:** In Colorado, fourth and fifth graders can obtain a Ski Passport packet good for 75 ski passes. Call and request an application form and program guidelines (see Contact Information). New Hampshire's fourth grade "Earn Your Turns" program provides free passes when kids complete a brief, school-related project. Participating "Ski New Hampshire" resorts also offer a "Take A Friend Program" that will land you a free lift ticket to any N.H. ski resort for getting a first-timer to sign up for a "Learn To" package.

♦ **California:** Squaw Valley, USA offers a special "ski five days, get the sixth day free" program. Be sure to contact them for all the details.

SAVE UP TO $1,000.00

Smokin!

Spring Skiing

Ski areas know that when people fail to see snow in their backyards, they won't venture to the hills. That means lift ticket prices often fall to 50 cents on the dollar and luxury rooms are available at Motel 6 prices. Call your favorite resorts and ask when prices drop.

◆ **Aspen:** America's premiere ski area begins melting in early April, and that's when you'll find the best bargains. The Wildwood Lodge, located at the base of Buttermilk Mountain, offers skiers an $82 package that includes lodging, lift tickets for any of the area's four mountains, and a daily breakfast buffet (not just toast and coffee here, folks) at their restaurant. Some seasonal restrictions may apply, so call ahead for reservations, and check the snow reports.

◆ **Pennsylvania:** More advanced skiers will find a bargain at Elk Mountain. Just present your season's pass to any mountain in the country and they'll give you an all-day lift ticket for $10. For those holding a Ski Card, a sort of AAA for skiers, you can get two lift tickets for the price of one.

◆ **Vermont:** At the end of March, skiers can enjoy a "Spring Break" special from Stowe Mountain Resort. For a cheap $79, skiers can stay at the lodge and receive free lift tickets. There's even the opportunity to ski free at Smuggler's Notch on the other side of the mountain.

Contact Information:

Colorado Passport Program (303) 866-9707

New Hampshire Earn Your Turns Program (800) 887-5464

Squaw Valley USA (888) 766-9321

The Wildwood Lodge, Aspen (800) 784-7166

Elk Mountain, Pennsylvania (570) 679-4400

>see also: Pay-Nothing yellow pages, skiing

Solve All Airport Troubles

Speak Up!

If you missed your flight, got bumped or cancelled, don't get mad, get educated. Learn the tricks of the Pay-Nothing Traveler, then put your seat backs in the full upright position and prepare for take-off.

When you miss your flight, never-ever call your travel agent and never-ever call the airline. Just skip the ticket counter and go directly to the boarding gate of the next flight or best connection to your destination. Politely explain every little detail of your day, whether it's the greasy sausage that upset your stomach or the nagging bunion that slowed your pace; tell the airline representative more than they need to know. Let them know they're your last hope of getting out of the airport. Blame everything on yourself and negotiate for sympathy. If you play your cards right, you'll either get on the next flight, get a good connection, or be charged a mere $75 for an entirely new ticket.

Good Idea
- Travel "on business!"
- Be an airline expert!
- Complain!

If you find yourself in a bind at the airport, maximum sympathy is the goal. If you have kids, bring your brood to the ticketing counter and explain the time and energy put into this vacation. Tell your new friends more than any one person really needs to know about you. Phrases like "our day began wrong when my car didn't start" and "this is my children's school vacation" will likely get the job done. Next, remove the kids from the scene and allow your helper to work in peace. It's important to stay silent. They know what time it is, and they know what you want.

Ticket agents have incredible power to provide you with new flights, free roundtrip tickets, hotel rooms with connecting rooms for the kids, dinners, breakfast, toiletries, and even on-the-spot checks delivered to competing airlines to soften your travel blows. Be nice, and watch your problems disappear.

SAVE UP TO $1000.00

Stay Free,
and Give Peace a Chance

The Pay-Nothing Traveler is most peaceful and happy when someone else is picking up the tab. That's why Servas, an organization founded to strengthen global peace efforts, brought a genuine tear to the PayNada.com Editors' eyes.

Travelers who successfully go through the organization's application process pay a $65 membership fee and are then welcome to visit any other member and stay up to two nights—on the house. And with more than 14,000 hosts in over 130 countries currently in the program, it's high time to travel the world, experience new cultures, and meet new friends.

Contact Information:
Servas 11 John Street, Suite 407
New York, NY 10038
(212) 267-0252
<www.servas.org>

SAVE UP TO $1000.00

Contact Information:

Accommodations Express
(800) 444-7666

California Reservations
(800) 576-0003

American Airlines
(800) 237-7981

American West Airlines
(800) 235-9292

Auto Driveaway Company
310 South Michigan Avenue
Chicago, IL 60604
(800) 346-2277

Bare Associates International
(800) 296-6699
<www.rhscorp.com>

Cash Saver
(888) 327-8971
(702) 642-5556
<www.lasvegascomps.
com/LasVegas.htm>

Colorado Passport Program
(303) 866-9707

Continental Airlines
(800) 441-1135

The Council on International Educational
Exchange
205 E. 42nd Street
New York, NY 10017
(888) 268-6245

Council Travel
(800) 2-COUNCIL
[226-8624]
<www.counciltravel.com>

Delta Airlines
(800) 221-1212

Elderhostel
(877) 426-8056
<www.elderhostel.org>

Elk Mountain, Pennsylvania
(570) 679-4400

Hilton Hotels
(800) 445-8667

Holiday Inn
(800) 465-4329

72

Contact Information:

Hotel Plus
(800) 235-0909

Hotel Reservations Network
(800) 964-6835

Hyatt Hotels
(800) 233-1234

International Air Coupon Exchange
(800) 558-0053

The LPGA
(904) 274-6200
<www.lpga.com>

The National Hurricane Center/Tropical
Prediction Center
(305) 227-4470
<www.nhc.noaa.gov>

New Hampshire
Earn Your Turns Program
(800) 887-5464
The PGA
(904) 285-3700
<http://pgatour.com>

Radisson Hotels
(800) 333-3333

Ritz-Carlton Hotels
(800) 241-3333

The Room Exchange
(800) 846-7000

Shop and Check
PO Box 740045
Atlanta, GA 30374
(800) 669-6526
<www.shopncheck.com>

Servas
11 John Street, Suite 407
New York, NY 10038
(212) 267-0252
<www.servas.org>

The State Department
(888) 987-0987

The Stowe Area Association
(802) 253-7321
<www.gostowe.com>

Squaw Valley USA
(888) 766-9321

The Wildwood Lodge
(800) 784-7166

Chapter 4

Save up to $10,000.00

Get Paid to Vacation

Free

Speak Up!

Word of mouth is magic in the travel industry. That's why Pay-Nothing Travelers gather friends and put trips together for cash-less passage.

Here's how it works: There are a few travel companies that seek out people who have the social skills to organize friends and acquaintances for vacationing. STS is a company that specializes in spring break vacations. Under their guidelines, they would love to pay your expenses, plus give you a percentage of the take if their booking targets are met.

◆ Emerald Cruises: They're the free cruise experts. Organize a group, and you'll earn a free berth. Plus, your whole crew will benefit from an across the board 20-30% savings.

◆ GalaxSea: Get 15 or more people to sign up for a cruise and your room, board, and airfare will all be free.

◆ Princess Cruise Lines: All it takes is nine people on a seven-day cruise to earn free passage on the Love Boat. Ten-day cruises require 14 people.

◆ Celebrity and Carnival Cruises: Each cruise line lets the 16th person (you) stay for free when 15 (your prey) are booked for any of their cruises.

◆ Myrtle Beach Connection offers an incredible free golf vacation for anyone putting together a group of 20 or more putters. The accommodations are at Bay Tree Condos, within short distance of over 90 primo golf courses.

Contact Information:

Emerald Cruises	(888) 313-8883
GalaxSea	(408) 363-4000
Princess Cruise Lines	(800) 774-6237
Celebrity Cruise Lines	(800) 437-3111
Carnival Cruise Lines	(800) 327-9501
Myrtle Beach Connection	(800) 742-2091

SAVE UP TO $10,000.00

Become a
Worldly Air Courier

Smokin!

I f packing your bags is more of a hassle than returning videos, consider the carry-on route. Just offer your baggage space to some Fortune 500 company. This award winning move is a sacred secret of the Pay-Nothing Traveler, and it will save you a small fortune of your own.

This isn't like sneaking baboons out of Borneo; you just make sure time-sensitive materials clear customs quickly. Smart couriers land flights to places like Rio de Janeiro, Mexico City, and Hong Kong for as little as $99.

Secrets That Apply
- Travel write!
- Travel "on business!"
- Be an airline expert!
- Volunteer!

The Air Courier Association acts as a sort of clearinghouse for the industry. There are a few catches. First, you cannot check luggage as your baggage space is being sacrificed. Second, trips are often booked at the last minute, making planning difficult. But becoming a courier is not hard work. Companies know that they are not dealing with professionals, and they normally have someone meet you at both ends of the trip to ensure all goes well. While being an air courier isn't for everyone, it's a great way to get out of town for a few days and have a real adventure in an exotic, foreign land.

Contact Information:

The Air Courier Association   (800) 282-1202
<www.aircourier.org>

The International Association of Air Travel Companies   (561) 582-8320
<www.courier.org>

Now Voyager   (212) 431-1616
<www.nowvoyagertravel.com>

SAVE UP TO $10,000.00

Travel Write
Your Way Anywhere

W e think professional travel writers are just a bunch of mortgage-avoiding cheapskates trying to finish their lousy novels. But we have to hand it to them—they know how to Pay-Nothing to travel. That's why our writers went undersea and over land to learn their trade. And by promising to read each Great American Novel—and forcing it upon our publisher—we learned, practiced, and perfected the scoop.

Being a travel writer entitles the Pay-Nothing Traveler to everything from discounts at major resorts to comped rooms and meals. The savings can be huge. To become a travel writer, the Pay-Nothing Traveler only needs an assignment from a publication and a destination that will accept them. To get started, here are a few ideas for obtaining an assignment:

- ◆ Your Church or Synagogue Newsletter
- ◆ Your Company Newsletter
- ◆ Your Local Paper
- ◆ Your Local Free Paper
- ◆ Any Magazines
- ◆ Any Newspaper

Special Report

Call for the report "Anybody's Travel Writing Crash Course." 1-877-Pay-Nothing

Continued ▶

SAVE UP TO $10,000.00

Smokin!

Free

Believe us: lining up an assignment is one of the easiest tasks in this book. To find a publisher, visit the Writer's Guideline Database or check out our suggestions.

Speak Up!

Remember: advertising is expensive. You are doing a great service to hotels, restaurants, even entire cities by even offering to write an article about them, regardless of your publication's size. Now that you've got an assignment, write a letter to your destination. Let them know who you are, where you work, and which publication you write for. Next, describe your story, when you're planning to visit, and how many people read your publication.

Once the letter's mailed, give it about a week to arrive and get read. Now it's time to call your destination. Always try to speak with management, and always restate the information in the letter. Once approved, the Pay-Nothing Traveler is on their way to great savings every time they take a vacation.

Contact Information:

The Writer's Network
<www.writersnetwork.com>

>see also: Pay-Nothing yellow pages, travel writer

SAVE UP TO $10,000.00

Forget Your Wallet, We're Shipping Out

Speak Up! *Free*

Smokin!

T he cruise line industry is growing faster than waistlines after midnight buffet, and its due in part to the popularity of "Titanic." Today, there are over 100 luxury liners, and an average of 10 being built each year. To prevent *Mutiny on the Bounty*, entertainment directors routinely pack the day's events with seminars, entertainers and movies. This is where the Pay-Nothing Traveler becomes the Seminar Leader.

Nearly every major cruise line is willing to welcome you (and a guest) aboard if you offer something as simple as a 45-minute lecture on any subject that interests you. You don't need to be an experienced or well-known speaker. There are hundreds of topics you can present, including cooking, arts & crafts, business seminars, and golf. Basically, if you can parlay your hobby into a brief seminar that gets accepted, you and your guest are on the boat. There may be a small charge for guests—usually about 10% of the normal berth. The Pay-Nothing Traveler can even translate languages or become a male dance host (dancing with single women) to win free passage.

Great Tip

• Travel write!
• Be an expert!

Contact Information:

>see also: Pay-Nothing yellow pages, cruises and entertainment, booking

SAVE UP TO $10,000.00

Take a Last Minute Cruise

P ay-Nothing Travelers know that making last-minute reservations via a cruise consolidator is the first class ticket to getting 30-50% knocked off the regular ticket price.

Once connected with a consolidator, these pros will get you aboard the cruise of your dreams while leaving hundreds of greenbacks in your pocket. A favorite among PayNada.com Editors, you give up nothing but price. Enjoy every bit of the luxury of your chosen cruise line without the high cost.

Secrets That Apply
• Travel Write!

Contact Information:

Cruise Line	(800) 327-3021
Cruise.com	(888) 289-7187
<www.cruise.com>	
Spur of the Moment Cruises	(800) 343-1991
Sunburst Cruises	(800) 398-0115
<www.DrCruise.com>	
White Travel	(800) 547-4790

>see also: Pay-Nothing yellow pages, cruises

82

SAVE UP TO $10,000.00

Watch Kids in Eden

Here's one exclusively for the female Pay-Nothing Traveler: if your schedule is flexible, you have at least one year of child care experience, and a couple people who will serve as professional references, pack your bags. You're hired for Club Med's short-term Au Pair program.

In exchange for eyeing little darlings for a few hours a day, you'll get free room and board, and your evenings are free to mosey around the resort property. This program is especially good for students looking for a free spring break or summer vacation.

Contact Information:

Club Med
(800) 258-2633

SAVE UP TO $10,000.00

Get an All-Expense Paid Caribbean Vacation

Free

Smokin!

Speak Up!

T hink of the dumbest thing you've ever done, and now imagine getting paid for it. That's the level of talent often displayed at all-inclusive resorts throughout the Caribbean. It's also why Pay-Nothing Travelers, those magicians of wallet-hiding, point their wands down south for free, all-expense paid trips.

Sandals resort in Jamaica, for example, is always looking for basic entertainment to keep the beach bums happy after sunset. For a mere 45-minute set of music, comedy, magic, or any Vaudevillian talent, Sandals will actually fly the Pay-Nothing Traveler to their Jamaican resort and comp the hotel room, meals, drinks, and resort amenities. And you have your days off!

Secrets That Apply
- Be an expert!
- Volunteer!

Club Med is also a company highly committed to entertainment. If you can sing, dance, or have any sort of interesting talent, then there may be a free ride for you, too. Individual resort managers are always open to new ideas, so offer up your proposal, videotape, and reference list. If your proposal is of interest, chances are very high that you will be offered free room, board, and use of facilities in exchange for a few performances.

Contact Information:

Sandals	(876) 979-9130
Club Med	(800) 258-2633
<clubmed.com>	

84

SAVE UP TO $10,000.00

Swap Your Home
for a Swiss Chalet

I f you break down international travel to its basic costs, you'll inevitably find that most of your money is spent on sleeping and eating. Pay-Nothing Travelers who own homes avoid these costs by routinely taking advantage of one of various house swapping services.

Secrets That Apply
• *Volunteer!*

Just join one of several, excellent house swap organizations (about $50 bucks) and get your house listed. Members can flip through the services' catalogs, note any homes or destinations that would make for a prime vacation, and get swapping. You'll receive lots of inquiries about your pad too, but you'll also have ultimate say over any would-be guests.

Ready to swap? It's a good idea to lay some house rules based upon your personal preferences, such as no-smoking zones and the use of your food staples. House swappers exist in most western countries, and the homes can be quite spectacular. Get on these lists and live large while saving some serious cash.

Contact Information:

Home Link
(800) 638-3841
<www.conch.net/~homelink>

Invented City
(800) 788-2489
<www.invented-city.com>

SunSwap
<www.sunswap.com>

SAVE UP TO $10,000.00

Travel Free
for Being an Expert

Speak Up! **Free**

Smokin!

Ⅰf your idea of international travel is two loops around Epcot, it's time to find a new magic carpet. Just lecture on any one topic from economics to sports, and join the many Pay-Nothing Travelers already "on the circuit." Astonishingly, the United States Information Agency recruits and sends people all over the world to deliver speeches on a multitude of subjects. And they'll cart you around in style.

Now, let's get this straight. We're talking about an all-inclusive vacation for nada, zilch, zero. Plus, you can probably call it business for tax purposes. If chosen, you can bank on traveling to places you would normally never consider, such as the Far East or even Africa. Put your money toward bringing a companion, and you've got yourself a deal.

Good idea

• *Teach English!*

Contact Information:

American Experts Overseas Lecture Tour,
Office of Thematic Programs
United States Information Agency
301 Fourth Street SW, 4th floor N.
Washington, DC 20547
(202) 619-4764

86

SAVE UP TO $10,000.00

Fly the Upstarts: They Try Harder

Easy

With major airlines continuing to raise their prices, upstart airlines provide Pay-Nothing Travelers with just the right ticket. For coast to coast travel at maximum savings and minimal hassle, no one beats scrappy Southwest Airlines, but there are other incredible savings to be had at ticket counters across the country. Check out the following sample of low-cost airlines and the general regions they service.

♦ AirTrans: The South, including Florida and Texas, and the Midwest, including Ohio and Michigan.

Special Report
Call for the guide "Low-Cost Airlines: Full Disclosure." 1-877-Pay-Nothing

♦ American TransAir: In addition to Florida, Texas, and New York, American TransAir services western states, and Hawaii. They also service Mexico, the Bahamas, Jamaica, and Ireland.

♦ Frontier Airlines: In addition to Atlanta, Baltimore, and Boston, Frontier Airlines services most western and mid-western states.

♦ Horizon Air: The Northwest section of the US, including Montana and Idaho. Horizon Air also services several Canadian provinces.

♦ MetroJet: The South, New England, and some mid-western states.

♦ Midway Airlines: The South, New England, and some mid-western states.

♦ Reno Air: The West and Anchorage, Alaska and Vancouver, British Columbia.

Continued

◆ SouthWest: Service across the US and Canada.

◆ Sunjet: Florida, Atlanta, Chicago, Detroit, Newark, and New York City.

◆ Tower Air: In addition to Los Angeles, San Francisco, Miami, and Fort Lauderdale, Tower Air services San Juan, Puerto Rico; Paris, France; Athens, Greece; and Tel-Aviv, Israel.

◆ Vanguard: In addition to Atlanta and Pittsburgh, Vanguard services mid-western states.

Contact Information:

AirTrans
(800) 825-8538
<www.airtran.com>

American TransAir
(800) 225-2995
<www.ata.com>

American West Airlines
(800) 235-9292

Frontier Airlines
(800) 432-1359
<www.frontierairlines.com>

Horizon Air
(800)547-9308
<www.horizonair.com>

MetroJet
(888) 638-7653
<www.usairways.com>

Midway Airlines
(800) 446-4392
<www.midwayair.com>

Reno Air
(800) 736-6247
<www.renoair.com>

SouthWest
(800)435-9792
<www.southwest.com>

Sunjet
(800) 478-6538
<www.sunjet.com>

Tower Air
(800) 348-6937

Vanguard
(800) 826-4827

SAVE UP TO $10,000.00

Join These Partnership Networks

Easy *Free*

For Pay-Nothing Travelers, here's a sample of the best connected partnership programs we've found. Give them a call or visit their websites for more information that will save you suitcases full of money.

AIRLINES

American AAdvantage
(800) 882-8880
<www.AA.com>

Northwest WorldPerks
(800)447-3757
<www.nwa.com/freqfly/index.html>

Continental OnePass
(800) 621-7467
<www.onepass.com>

HOTELS

Hyatt Gold Passport
(800) 544-9288
<www.goldpassport.com>

BestWestern Gold Crown Club
(800) 237-8483
<www.bestwestern.com>

Marriott Rewards
(800) 249-3276
< www.marriottrewards.com>

CREDIT CARDS

Amex Membership Rewards
(800) 297-3276
<www.americanexpress.com/rewards/programs/>

Diners Club Rewards
(800) 234-4034
<www.citibank.com/dinersus/clbrwds/clbframe.htm>

Join the Best Travel Clubs

Y our PayNada.com Editors went on a serious research binge to find the best travel club values for the buck. We decided, though, if we're going to carry one of those annoying travel club credit cards, we'd better be saving more green than the Sierra Club.

◆ MemberWorks Online: Sign up for their introductory, 30-day membership ($69.95 per year), and you'll receive two, free roundtrip airline tickets. You can even cancel your membership at any time after the 30 days and receive a prorated refund. Once a member, you can expect discounts of up to 50% at more than 150,000 hotels in over 120 countries.

◆ Entertainment Publications: They sell a terrific coupon book ($39) packed with specials for over 200 cities worldwide. These books consistently knock 50% off hotels and 20% off on restaurants, stores, car rentals, sporting events, and other attractions.

◆ Encore Traveler: These folks offer a Preferred Traveler card for $59 per year that boasts guaranteed savings of up to 65% off 18,000 hotels world-wide. You can also expect up to 25% discounts on car rentals and a variety of savings on your vacation chow.

◆ Quest International Corporation: For a $99 membership fee, you can get 50% off at over 2,100 hotels (with 25% off the hotel's restaurants), as well as discounts on cruises, condominiums, and airfare.

Contact Information:

MemberWorks Online	<www.memberworks.com>
Entertainment Publications	(800) 477-3234
Encore Traveler	(800) 638-8976
Quest International Corporation	(800) 560-4100

SAVE UP TO $10,000.00

Join All Frequent Flyer Programs

Easy *Free*

$\mathbf{I}$t only takes a few minutes, and the benefits are enormous. That's why Pay-Nothing Travelers just say "Yes, please" when given an application form. While American Express Membership Miles wins our vote for convenience and versatility, a few other road rules should be noted.

The Pay-Nothing Traveler should consider using a travel agent when making reservations. Travel agents typically hate awards tickets because they earn zero commission on them. But airlines are notorious for frequent flyer roadblocks (blackout days, cryptic pin codes, and mystery fees), so this is a good time to let your travel agent earn your future business.

Secrets That Apply
- Travel "on business!"
- Upgrade constantly!

Contact Information:

American Express Membership Miles
(800) 528-4800
<www.frequentfliers.com>

Alaska Airlines Mileage Plan
(800) 654-5669
<www.alaska-air.com>

American Airlines AAdvantage
(800) 882-8880
<www.AA.com>

Delta Sky Miles
(800) 323-2323
<www.delta-air.com>

Gigantic Savings From AmEx

I t's difficult for the Pay-Nothing Traveler to understand why anyone needs a credit card other than an American Express. With no interest, zillions of locations, and great programs, the following programs complete the pie.

◆ Figure out a way to obtain their Personal Platinum card, which is really a piece of plastic painted silver with an impressive rap. Stomach the $300 annual fee fast—dessert's comin'. The program allows for a free "companion ticket" for every international, first, or business-class flight—a true gold mine feature. Plus, the insurance on this silver spoon is impressive. Cardholders injured abroad are eligible for free Med-Evac transportation from, say, Dr. Iguana's Hut of Voodoo to Mass General's private wing. Throw in free rental car and room upgrades at over 360 hotels, and, well, where do we sign?

◆ The AmEx Optima Card and Continental Airlines have teamed up to aggressively court the college market with a phenomenal program. Students paying with AmEx can receive 12 vouchers from Continental Airlines good for coast-to-coast flights. Cost: $269.

◆ American Express Membership Miles is one of several credit card programs with lots of airline, hotel and rent-a-car partners. Every dollar spent can be transferred to miles via touch-tone phone. Consider putting inevitable high-ticket items, such as automobiles and wedding expenses, on the card. Besides the bill, you'll surely gain enough good-dog points for a couple of roundtrip business class tickets to better-better lands.

◆ Finally, AmEx airport kiosks dispense cash in the only language they understand: American Express Card-ese. That's good news when an overseas ATM chomps your cash card or spits out stupid lies like your account is overdrawn (we know, it can't be). The program requires prior sign-up, so call AmEx for complete details.

SAVE UP TO $10,000.00

Contact Information:

The Air Courier Association
(800) 282-1202
<www.aircourier.org>

AirTrans
(800) 825-8538
<www.airtran.com>

Alaska Airlines Mileage Plan
(800) 654-5669
<www.alaska-air.com>

American Airlines AAdvantage
(800) 882-8880
<www.AA.com>

American Experts
Overseas Lecture Tour,
Office of Thematic Programs
US Information Agency
301 Fourth Street SW,
4th floor N.
Washington, DC 20547
(202) 619-4764

American Express
<www.americanexpress.com>

American Express
Membership Miles
(800) 528-4800

American TransAir
(800) 225-2995
<www.ata.com>

American West Airlines
(800) 235-9292

Carnival Cruise Lines
(800) 327-9501

Celebrity Cruise Lines
(800) 437-3111

Club Med
(800) 258-2633
<clubmed.com>

Cruise.com
(888) 289-7187
<www.cruise.com>

Cruise Line
(800) 327-3021

Delta Sky Miles
(800) 323-2323
<www.delta-air.com>

Emerald Cruises
(888) 313-8883

Encore Traveler
(800) 638-8976

Entertainment Publications
(800) 477-3234

<www.frequentfliers.com>

Frontier Airlines
(800) 432-1359
<www.frontierairlines.com>

GalaxSea(408) 363-4000

Home Link
(800) 638-3841
<www.conch.net/~homelink>

Horizon Air
(800)547-9308
<www.horizonair.com>

The International Association of
Air Travel Companies
220 South Dixie Highway #3 PO
Box 1349Lake Worth, FL 33460
Phone: (561) 582-8320
Fax: (561) 582-1581

Contact Information:

Invented City
(800) 788-2489
<www.invented-city.com>

MemberWorks Online
<www.memberworks.com>

MetroJet
(888) 638-7653
<www.usairways.com>

Midway Airlines
(800) 446-4392
<www.midwayair.com>

Myrtle Beach Connection
(800) 742-2091

Now Voyager
(212) 431-1616
<www.nowvoyagertravel.com>

Princess Cruise Lines
(800) 774-6237

Quest International Corporation
(800) 560-4100

Reno Air
(800) 736-6247
<www.renoair.com>

Sandals
(876) 979-9130

SouthWest
(800)435-9792
<www.southwest.com>

Spur of the Moment Cruises
(800) 343-1991

Sunburst Cruises
(800) 398-0115
<www.DrCruise.com>

Sunjet
(800) 478-6538
<www.sunjet.com>

SunSwap
<www.sunswap.com>

Tower Air
(800) 348-6937

Vanguard
(800) 826-4827

White Travel
(800) 547-4790

The Writer's Network
<www.writersnetwork.com>

SAVE UP TO $10,000.00

Airlines

AirTrans
(800) 825-8538
<www.airtran.com>

American Airlines
(800) 237-7981
<www.AA.com>

American TransAir
(800) 225-2995
<www.ata.com>

American West Airlines
(800) 235-9292

Continental Airlines
(800) 441-1135
<www.continental.com>

Delta Airlines
(800) 221-1212
<www.delta-air.com>

Frontier Airlines
(800) 432-1359
<www.frontierairlines.com>

Horizon Air
(800)547-9308
<www.horizonair.com>

MetroJet
(888) 638-7653
<www.usairways.com>

Midway Airlines
(800) 446-4392
<www.midwayair.com>

Reno Air
(800) 736-6247
<www.renoair.com>

SouthWest
(800)435-9792
<www.southwest.com>

Sunjet
(800) 478-6538
<www.sunjet.com>

Tower Air
(800) 348-6937

United Airlines
<www.ual.com>

US Airways
<www.usairways.com>

Vanguard
(800) 826-4827

Airlines, Air Courier

The Air Courier Association
(800) 282-1202
<www.aircourier.org>

International Association of Air Travel Companies
220 South Dixie Highway #3
PO Box 1349
Lake Worth, FL 33460
Phone: (561) 582-8320
Fax: (561) 582-1581
<www.courier.org>

Now Voyager
(212) 431-1616
<www.nowvoyagertravel.com>

Airlines, Coupon Broker

International Air Coupon Exchange
(800) 558-0053

Airlines, Frequent Flyer

<www.frequentfliers.com>

Auto Delivery

Auto Driveaway Company
310 South Michigan Avenue
Chicago, IL 60604
(800) 346-2277

Camping

National Park Services Headquarters
Office of Public Inquiries,
Room 1013
US Department of the Interior
1849 C Street, NW
PO Box 37127
Washington, DC 20013-7127

National Forestry Service and Bureau of Land Management
<www.recreation.gov>

Chamber of Commerce

Global Chamber of Commerce Listing
<http://www.g77tin.org
_www.g77tin.org>

Cruises

Carnival Cruise Lines
(800) 777-9999
(800) 327-9501

Celebrity Cruise Lines
(800) 437-3111

Emerald Cruises
(888) 313-8883

GalaxSea
(408) 363-4000

Norwegian Cruise Lines
(800) 327-7030

Princess Cruise Lines
(800) 774-6237

Cruises, Consolidators

Cruise.com
(888) 289-7187
<www.cruise.com>

Cruise Line
(800) 327-3021

Spur of the Moment Cruises
(800) 343-1991

Sunburst Cruises
(800) 398-0115
<www.DrCruise.com>

White Travel
(800) 547-4790

Credit Cards

American Express
<www.americanexpress.com>

Membership Rewards
(800) 279-3276

Personal Platinum Cards
(800) 525-3355

Student cards
(800) 582-5823

ATM services
(800) CASH NOW [227-4669]

Diners Club Rewards
(800)234-4034
<www.citibank.com/dinersus/
clbrwds/clbframe.htm>

Dining Cards

IGT Charge Card
(800) 444-8872

Premier Dining Card
(800) 346-3241

Transmedia Card
(800) 422-5090

Entertainment, Booking

Karp Enterprises, Inc.
1999 University Drive, Suite 213
Coral Springs, FL 33701

Golf

The LPGA
(904) 274-6200
<www.lpga.com>

Myrtle Beach Connection
(800) 742-2091

The PGA
(904) 285-3700
<www.pgatour.com>

Government Offices

Dahlonega, Georgia Welcome Center
(706) 864-3711

The American Experts Overseas Lecture Tour Office of Thematic Programs United States Information Agency
301 Fourth Street SW, 4th floor N.
Washington, DC 20547
(202) 619-4764

Department of Agriculture
(800) 535-4555

The National Hurricane Center/Tropical Prediction Center
(305) 227-4470
<www.nhc.noaa.gov>

National Park Services Headquarters
Office of Public Inquiries,
Room 1013
US Department of the Interior
1849 C Street, NW
PO Box 37127
Washington, DC 20013-7127

National Forestry Service and Bureau of Land Management
<www.recreation.gov>

The State Department
(888) 987-0987

The US Capitol
(202) 225-3121

US Geological Survey

Information Services
(800) 435-7627

Washington, DC Convention and Visitor's Association
(202) 789-7000
<www.washington.org>

Home Swap

Home Link
(800) 638-3841
<www.conch.net/~homelink>

Invented City
(800) 788-2489
<www.invented-city.com>

SunSwap (a web-based service)
<www.sunswap.com>

Limousine Service

SuperShuttle
<www.supershuttle.com>

Lodging

Lodging, Bed & Breakfasts

The Evergreen Bed & Breakfast Club
PO Box 1430
Falls Church, VA 22041
(800) 962-2392

Lodging, Consolidators

Accommodations Express
(800) 444-7666

California Reservations
(800) 576-0003

Hotel Plus
(800) 235-0909

Hotel Reservations Network
(800) 964-6835

The Room Exchange
(800) 846-7000

Lodging, Dormitories

The Campus Lodging Guide
B&J Publications
PO Box 5486
Fullerton, CA 92635
(800) 525-6633

Lodging, Fraternities and Sororities

Greek Pages
<www.greekpages.com/LocalsOnline/index.htm>

Greek Zone
<www.greekzone.com>
(317) 872-1112

Lodging, Hotels

Hilton Hotels
(800) 445-8667

Holiday Inn
(800) 465-4329

Hyatt Hotels
(800) 233-1234

Radisson Hotels
(800) 333-3333

Ritz-Carlton Hotels
(800) 241-3333

Lodging, Programs

BestWestern
Gold Crown Club
(800) 237-8483
<www.bestwestern.com>

Hyatt Gold Passport
(800) 544-9288
<www.goldpassport.com>

Marriott Rewards
(800) 450-4442
< www.marriottrewards.com>

Lodging, All-Inclusive Resorts

Sandals, Jamaica
(876) 979-9130

Club Med
(800) 258-2633

Lodging, Resorts—The Caribbean

The Bahamian Chamber of Commerce
(242) 322-2145

Friends of the Bahamas
<www.members.tripod.com/
~amahab/index.html>

Lodging, Resorts—Hawaiian Resorts

For a complete listing:
(888) 403-1475
<www.visitor center.com>

<www.hawaiihotels.com>

Lodging, Resorts—The Poconos

The Pocono Chamber of Commerce
(570) 421-4433
<www.poconochamber.com>

"This Week" magazine
<www.thisweek.net>

Lodging, Resorts—Vermont

Stowe Area Association
(802) 253-7321
<www.gostowe.com>

Lodging, Resources

AAA Tour book
(800) 222-4357

Mobil Travel Guide
3225 Gallows Road, Suite 7D0407
Fairfax, VA 22037
<www.mobil.com/travel>

Medical Assistance

Ask-a-Nurse
(800) 535-1111

Department of Agriculture
(800) 535-4555

People's Medical Society
(800) 624-8773

Museums

High Museum
(404) 733-4400

**The Boston Museum
of Fine Arts**
(617) 267-9300

**The Chicago Museum of
Contemporary Art**
(312) 280-2660

The Harvard Museums
(617) 495-9400

**The Institute of
Contemporary Art, Boston**
(617) 266-5152

**Museum of Modern Art,
San Francisco**
(415) 357-4000

**The Peabody Essex
Museum**
(978) 745-1876

The Seattle Art Museum
(206) 654-3100

**The Washington, DC Bureau
of Tourism**
(202) 789-7000

Online Booking Companies

<www.1travel.com>

<www.Bestfares.com>

<www.cheaptickets.com>

<www.expedia.com>

<www.frequentfliers.com>

<www.priceline.com>

<www.travelcity.com>

Organizations

**The Council on
International Educational
Exchange**
205 E. 42nd Street
New York, NY 10017
(888) 268-6245

The Council Travel
(800) 2-COUNCIL [226-8624]
<www.counciltravel.com>

Elderhostel
(877) 426-8056
<www.elderhostel.org>

Servas

11 John Street, Suite 407
New York, NY 10038
(212) 267-0252
<www.servas.org>

Rental Car Companies

Alamo
(800) 327-9633

Auto Europe
(800) 223-5555

Avis
(800) 331-1212

Budget
(800) 527-0700

Eurodollar, Ltd.
(800) 800-6000

Hertz
(800) 654-3131

Thrifty
(800) FORCARS [367-2277]

Value
(800) GOVALUE [468-2583]

Secret Shopper

Bare Associates International
(800) 296-6699
<www.rhscorp.com>

Shop and Check
PO Box 740045
Atlanta, GA 30374
(800) 669-6526.
<www.shopncheck.com>

Shipping

Greyhound Package Express
(800) 739-5020

Mail Boxes Etc.
<www.mbe.com>

United Parcel Service
(800) 742-5877

Skiing

Colorado Passport Program
(303) 866-9707

Elk Mountain, Pennsylvania
(570) 679-4400

Killington, Vermont
(800) 372-2007

New Hampshire Earn Your Turns Program
(800) 887-5464

Squaw Valley USA
(888) 766-9321

Sunday River, Maine
(800) 543-2754

Snowbird, Utah
(800) 453-3000

Stowe Area Association
(802) 253-7321
<www.gostowe.com>.

Vail/Beaver Creek, Colorado
(800) 525-2257

The Wildwood Lodge, Aspen
(800) 784-7166

Tickets

BosTix
www.boston.com/artsboston/

The Hit Show Club
630 Ninth Avenue
New York, NY 10036
(212) 581-4211

New York Theatre Development Fund
1501 Broadway, Suite 2110
New York, NY 10036
Info line (212) 221-0013
Main office (212) 221-0885

On The House
(310) 392-7588

TKTS
Times Square (47th and Broadway)
2 World Trade Center

Tipping

The Maitre 'd Association
(702) 897-0971

Travel Agents

The American Society of Travel Agents
(703) 739-2782

AtoZ Travel
(314) 441-4447
<www.aatoztravel.com>

Travel Agencies

A-1 Travel
(800) 441-0008

STS
(800)648-4849
<www.ststravel.com>

Travel Clubs

Encore Traveler
(800) 638-8976

Entertainment Publications
(800) 477-3234

MemberWorks Online
<www.memberworks.com>

Quest International Corporation
(800) 560-4100

Travel Writing

The Writer's Network
<www.writersnetwork.com>

<www.lights.com/publisher>

Videos

Blockbuster Video
<www.blockbuster.com>

International Video Network
(800) 669-4486

Mentor Productions
(800) 521-5104

Index

N

O

P

R

S

Notes

Notes

Notes

Notes

Notes

Notes

Notes

Notes

Book and Report Order Form

Title   **Quantity**   **Amount**

1. Pay Nothing to Travel Anywhere You Like ($12.95)_____   _____

2. Special Reports($6.95 each. Please write in names from next page)

_____   _____   _____

_____   _____   _____

_____   _____   _____

_____   _____   _____

_____   _____   _____

_____   _____   _____

_____   _____   _____

                                        Total   _____

3. Book only shipping and handling
($2.95 1st book, $1.00 each additional)   _____

4. Special Report only shipping and handling
($1.00 1st report, $.50 each additional)   _____

                          Grand Total   _____

First Name   Last Name   Credit Card
                                        (Visa, Master Card, or American Express)

Street Address
                                        Credit Card Number

                                        Expiration Date

City   State   Zip Code   (Month/Year)   _____

Send your   **Great Pines Publishing**
payment to: **PO Box 973, Stowe, VT 05403**

Other Guides
Available From This Publisher

<u>Special Reports:</u>

- "How to Get Anything You Want"
- "Slash Hotel Rates Worldwide"
- "One Year Past Warranty? No Problem"
- "Low Cost Airlines: Full Disclosure"
- "Anybody's Travel Writing Crash Course"
- "Pay-Nothing for Super Bowl and Olympic Tickets"

Each Special Report is $6.95, plus S&H.
To order, call, toll free, 1-877-Pay-Nothing (729-6684).

<u>Other Books in the "Pay-Nothing" Series:</u>

- *Pay-Nothing to Spruce up Your Home*

- *Pay-Nothing for Anything Kids*

- *Pay-Nothing for Expert Financial Advice*

- *Pay-Nothing for Perfect Health Care*

- *Pay-Nothing to Travel France*
(other European cities available)

- *Pay-Nothing for Top Notch Education*

- *Pay-Nothing to Start, Fund, and Grow your Business*

- *Pay-Nothing to Beautify Your Garden*

- *Pay-Nothing for Everything*

All books $12.95 plus S&H.
To order, contact your local bookstore, or call, toll free,
1-877-Pay-Nothing (729-6684).